101 FACTS ABOUT

LIONS

Julia Barnes

Gareth Stevens Publishing
A WORLD ALMANAC EDUCATION GROUP COMPANY

Please visit our web site at: www.garethstevens.com
For a free color catalog describing Gareth Stevens Publishing's
list of high-quality books and multimedia programs,
call 1-800-542-2595 (USA) or 1-800-387-3178 (Canada).
Gareth Stevens Publishing's fax: (414) 332-3567.

Library of Congress Cataloging-in-Publication Data available upon request from publisher.
Fax (414) 336-0157 for the attention of the Publishing Records Department.

ISBN 0-8368-4037-2

This North American edition first published in 2004 by
Gareth Stevens Publishing
A World Almanac Education Group Company
330 West Olive Street, Suite 100
Milwaukee, WI 53212 USA

This U.S. edition copyright © 2004 by Gareth Stevens, Inc. Original edition © 2003 by First
Stone Publishing. First published in 2003 by First Stone Publishing, 4/5 The Marina,
Harbour Road, Lydney, Gloucestershire, GL15 5ET, United Kingdom. Additional end
matter © 2004 by Gareth Stevens, Inc.

First Stone Series Editor: Claire Horton-Bussey
First Stone Designer: Sarah Williams
Geographical consultant: Miles Ellison
Gareth Stevens Editor: Catherine Gardner

Printed in Hong Kong through Printworks Int. Ltd.

1 2 3 4 5 6 7 8 9 08 07 06 05 04

WHAT IS A PREDATOR?

Predators are nature's hunters, the creatures that must kill in order to survive. They come in all shapes and sizes, ranging from mighty lions and tigers to slithering snakes.

Although predators are different in many ways, they do have some things in common. All predators are necessary in the balance of nature. Predators keep the number of other animals under control, preventing disease and starvation. In addition, all predators adapted, or changed, to survive where they live. They developed special skills to find **prey** and kill it in the quickest, simplest way possible.

Lions are the top predators on the African plains. Built to handle big prey, lions have powerful, muscular bodies, sharp teeth and claws, and strong jaws. To gain an even greater advantage, they hunt in organized groups. Each lion in the group has its part to play in making the kill.

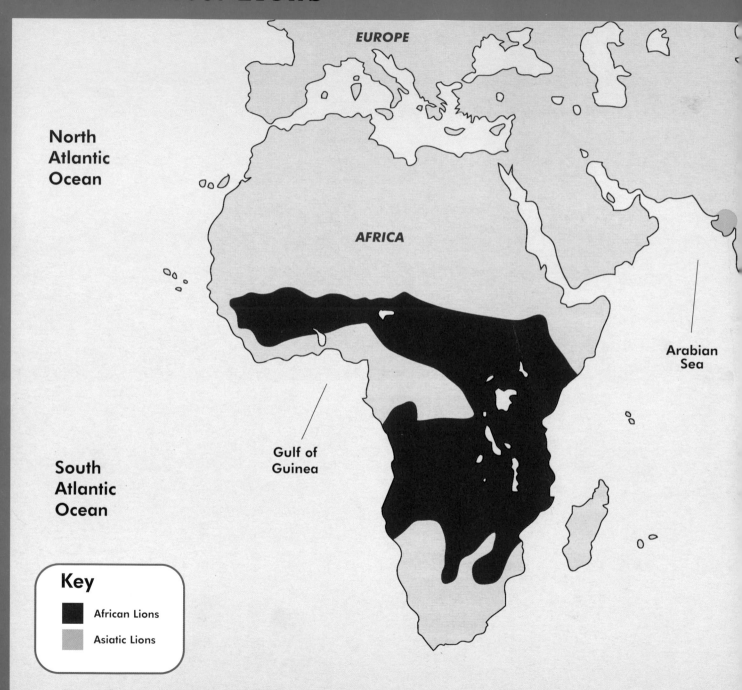

EUROPE

North
Atlantic
Ocean

AFRICA

Arabian
Sea

Gulf of
Guinea

South
Atlantic
Ocean

Key

African Lions

Asiatic Lions

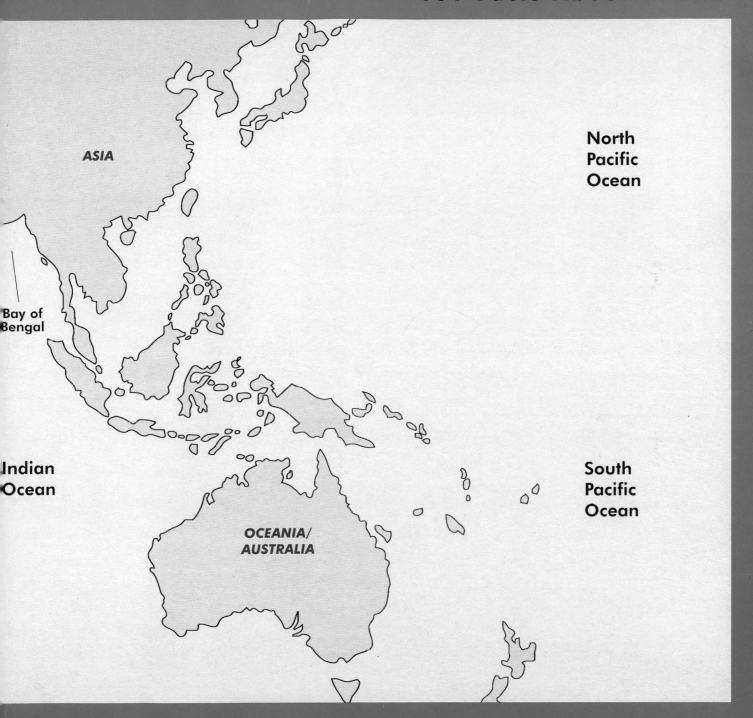

2 Lions, leopards, tigers, and jaguars are called big cats, which are wild cats that can roar. They have the same early ancestor, a small animal that lived sixty million years ago.

3 Animals that looked like today's lions developed about five million years ago. They lived in North America, Europe, Asia, and Africa, but they died out in most places.

1 The lion, a symbol of power and strength for thousands of years, is called the King of the Beasts. It is not the biggest cat, however. The tiger is larger.

4 Mountain lions of North and South America look like lions, but they really are cougars, or pumas.

5 Now, wild African lions live in parts of Africa, and a few Asiatic, or Indian, lions live in the Gir Protected Area in northwest India. (See pages 4-5.)

6 Asiatic lions and African lions look alike. Asiatic lions have smaller manes but thicker tufts of hair at the tips of their tails and elbows.

7 Lions are the only big cats with females that look different from males.

8 The male lion (left) is much bigger than the female. A male weighs about 400 pounds (180 kilograms). A **lioness** (below), or female, weighs closer to 275 pounds (125 kg).

9 A **mane** that grows on the head and shoulders (below) separates male lions from lionesses and separates lions from all other cats. The male lion is the only cat that has a mane.

10 Scientists think that a thick mane might protect a lion in a fight or show a lioness how healthy and strong the male is.

11 The mane color can be reddish brown or black, but often, the mane is the same color as the coat. The coat ranges from pale tan to dark yellowish brown.

12 The lion also has a tuft of hair at the tip of its tail that covers an area of tough skin. This area may once have been a kind of claw, but now it has no use.

13 The lion is the top predator in Africa. It has many different features that help it hunt efficiently in its **habitat**.

14 The lion's teeth (right) are powerful weapons. Long, pointed canine teeth in the front of its mouth hold down prey or slash another lion in a fight. The molar teeth in the back of the mouth cut meat.

15 The lion also uses its short, powerful jaws to clamp its teeth into prey more tightly.

16 The lion's claws are hooked and sharp. They are retractable, which means the lion pushes them out when needed but keeps them covered at other times.

17 The lion uses its claws for climbing, for wounding other animals, and for holding down prey.

fast for a long distance. It can go about 35 miles (56 kilometers) an hour (left) when it needs to sprint a short distance.

18 A hunter must have excellent eyesight. The lion, which likes to hunt in the cool evening hours, can see clearly in dim light and in the dark.

19 The lion is too big and heavy to run

20 **Wildebeests**, gazelles, and zebras, which are the lion's preferred foods, can outrun a lion over a long distance. They run as fast as 50 miles (80 km) per hour.

21 The lion is an expert at **stalking** its prey, advancing step by step and freezing if it is in danger of being spotted (right).

22 When the lion slinks close enough to a prey animal, it runs with an explosive burst of speed and pulls the animal down. The lion clamps its teeth on the animal's throat or muzzle to suffocate it.

23 Lionesses do most of the hunting for the **pride**. Females are smaller and more agile than males.

24 The male's huge mane makes it harder for him to hide from prey when he is hunting.

25 Despite the lion's tremendous hunting skills, most of its attempts to capture prey end in failure.

27 A lion hunts small prey on its own but works together with other lions (left) to tackle the biggest prey.

28 When they hunt in a group, the lionesses fan out and set up a formation around the prey animal. A lioness may stand in the same position in the formation during every hunt.

26 Sometimes, the prey animal roams out of the lion's range. Sometimes, it senses the lion's approach and escapes before the lion comes close. At other times, the prey animal dodges or outruns the attacking lion.

29 Slowly, the lionesses creep into a circle around their prey, blocking off all escape routes. Then they attack (right).

30 After a kill, the other lions in the family group join the feast. Male lions feed first. The lionesses move in next, and then the **cubs** take their turn.

31 Lions miss most of the prey they try to kill. They make a kill once every three or four days if food is plentiful but less often in harsh conditions.

32 When lions do have a meal, they gorge themselves, eating as much as they possibly can. They may not eat again for days.

33 A male lion is able to eat as much as 95 pounds (43 kg) of meat at a single sitting.

34 A lion kept in a zoo receives food on a regular schedule. It eats from 11 to 15 pounds (5 to 7 kg) of meat a day.

35 Lions usually hunt animals that weigh under 660 pounds (300 kg), such as antelopes or zebras. The only big cats that hunt in a group, lions can tackle an animal as large as a buffalo (below), which weighs more than 1,100 pounds (500 kg).

36 When food is hard to find, lions make do with smaller animals, such as **rodents**, hares, birds, and **reptiles**. Hungry lions even eat insects and fruit.

37 Most lions settle in grassy plains, open woodlands, or **scrublands**, but they can survive in sandy deserts, rocky mountains, or bamboo forests.

38 In the small Gir Protected Area in India, the Asiatic lion has found a home in the teak forests (right).

39 Whatever habitat the lion chooses, it must be a place that can support enough prey to feed all the lions in the pride.

40 As the top predator on the plains, the lion fears no other animals. Lions do compete with other animals, however, for their share of prey.

41 Leopards, cheetahs, and wild dogs hunt smaller prey animals, such as gazelles and warthogs. They cannot catch and kill larger animals.

42 Hyenas provide the stiffest competition for lions. A pack of hyenas hunting at night can bring down an animal as big as a zebra or a wildebeest.

43 Lions do not sit by and let hyenas take the prey. If lions find a pack of hyenas enjoying a meal, they chase away the hyenas and take over the feast.

44 Unlike the other big cats, lions are quite social and live in cooperative groups, or prides (above).

45 A pride is made up of several related females, their young cubs, and a group of males that may or may not be related.

46 A pride of African lions includes four to forty members. A typical pride has twelve lionesses, one to six males, and cubs.

47 In the Gir Protected Area, Asiatic lions form prides that include two to five adult females. Males join only to mate or to hunt a large animal.

48 A lion (right) gives information to pride members and to other lions by marking the land with his **urine** or **feces**. He also can make many different sounds, from grunts to roars.

49 The lion is famous for his mighty roar, which can be heard from a distance of 5 miles (8 km).

50 Roaring is the way lions keep in touch with members of the pride and warn other lions to stay away from them.

51 Sometimes, a whole pride joins in a loud chorus of roars. The group often roars after sundown, after a kill, and after eating.

water (left), and where it can enjoy the best tree branches for its daily rest.

54 Lions seem to take life easy. They rest about 80 percent of the day.

55 When they are not asleep, lions travel around the territory, patrol the borders, hunt, groom, or play together.

52 Each pride has its own **territory**. The size depends on the amount of prey and water available.

53 Within the territory, a lion knows where it can find shade in the heat of the day, where it can find

56 If prey is in short supply, the pride must travel farther to find food and may cover more than 5 miles (8 km) a day.

57 Within the pride, the lions work together to hunt and care for cubs. Rarely, fights break out as the lions begin to feed.

58 The adult lions in the pride take part in raising the cubs. Adults are patient with their active and playful cubs (right).

59 All the lionesses in a pride give birth to their cubs at about the same time. A few weeks after the cubs are born, the mothers take turns caring for all of the cubs in the pride.

60 While the lionesses hunt, one may stay behind to guard all of the cubs. She even allows cubs that are not her own to feed on her milk.

61 About fourteen weeks after **mating**, lionesses leave the pride and find safe, quiet places to give birth.

19

64 During the weeks just after birth, mothers keep their tiny cubs hidden in caves or narrow openings between rocks.

62 A lioness gives birth to as many as six cubs at once. Usually, two or three cubs are in a **litter**.

63 Lion cubs are tiny and helpless when they are born. They weigh less than 3 pounds (1.3 kg) at birth.

65 If a lioness senses danger, she moves all her cubs to a new hiding place. She carries them one by one in her teeth (left).

66 By the time the cubs are six weeks old, they have learned to walk and can follow their mother. Then they can join the pride.

67 The cubs grow fast and can eat meat when they are three months old. Their mother leads them to a kill, where they can take their share after the adults have had their fill.

68 Soon, the cubs join a hunt. At first, they follow and watch the adults. The cubs must learn many skills before they can help.

69 The cubs spend a lot of time playing (right). Their pretend fights and hunts prepare them for adult life.

70 All the lions in the pride take care of the cubs, but growing up in the wild is a risky business.

71 Cubs may die of diseases or starve to death in the years when food is tough to find.

72 Predators and food shortages kill many cubs. Eight out of ten cubs may die before age two.

73 Female cubs grow up in the pride (below). Most of them stay in the family group and add their own cubs as they grow older.

74 A lioness is able to start breeding after she is two years old.

75 Male cubs do not stay in the pride with their mothers. When males reach age two or three, the adult male lions force them out of the pride.

76 Often, a few male lions leave at the same time. A lone lion has a hard time killing enough food to survive.

77 A group of young males may form a team (right). They have no territory, so they must keep moving. They follow herds of prey and try to avoid the territories of stronger males.

78 After two years or so, the young male lions reach the peak of their physical strength. They find a pride led by older, weaker lions and attack. In this fight, the losers must leave or die.

79 The team of males that controls a pride attempts to defend it against attacking younger males. A pride's leaders may change every two or three years.

80 Fights between male lions (left) are often deadly. The lions attack each other with their sharp claws and fight until one of them dies or is so badly injured that he must give up and run away from the pride.

81 Male lions that take over a pride kill the youngest cubs.

82 After their cubs die, the females (right) are ready to mate again and raise cubs that are fathered by the new male lions at the head of the pride.

83 In the wild, a male lion may only live to be about twelve years old.

84 With the support of the pride, a lioness lives for as long as seventeen years. In the wild, diseases and fighting are two causes of early death.

85 Lions that are kept in zoos, safe from the dangers of the wild, have been known to live for up to twenty-five years.

86 The lion has little to fear from other animals, but it has much to fear from humans.

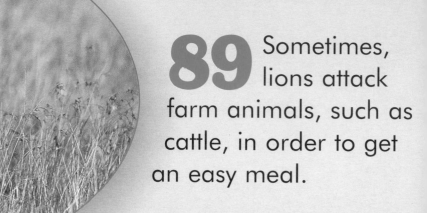

89 Sometimes, lions attack farm animals, such as cattle, in order to get an easy meal.

90 Farmers count on raising animals for their income. They see a lion (left) as a pest and a danger to their way of life.

87 As humans use up more land to build houses and raise crops, the wild land available for the lion to hunt shrinks.

91 People also worry that lions may kill them or their children.

88 Many prey animals need to have large areas where they can graze on plants. When they starve, lions go hungry, too.

92 In Africa, more than one hundred years ago, construction of a major railway had to be stopped after two lions killed dozens of the workers.

93 Humans would be an easy target, but lions (right) kill them only if there is no other prey to eat.

94 To protect their cattle, farmers put out a dead animal that has been poisoned. They know that the poisoned meat can kill a whole pride of lions that eats it.

95 Humans shoot lions for sport. They catch them in **snares** that they set to trap other animals. More and more, lions are not safe in the wild.

96 To protect the lions, people have set up **national parks** and **game reserves** (above). Hunting is restricted on this land.

97 The number of lions living in the wild is falling. Within the last two hundred years, the lion has no longer been able to live in the southern tip of Africa.

98 The Asiatic lion is in greater danger than the African lion. Only a very few Asiatic lions are left.

99 Today, the Asiatic lion (right) makes

a home only in the Gir Protected Area in India. About 250 to 300 lions live in this park.

100 Some zoos are part of breeding programs that encourage lions to have cubs in the zoo. Asiatic cubs born in zoos may help boost the number of lions in India.

101 African lions are not yet endangered, but people need to leave enough land on Earth for lions.

 # Glossary

cubs: the young of some animals.

feces: animal droppings.

game reserves: areas for wildlife where hunting is not allowed.

habitat: the place where an animal naturally lives and grows.

lioness: a female lion.

litter: a group of young born to the same mother at the same time.

mane: the hair around the male lion's neck.

mating: coming together of a male and female to produce young.

national parks: a country's large wildlife parks and natural areas where hunting is forbidden.

predators: animals that kill other animals for food.

prey: the animal a predator picks to hunt and kill.

pride: a group of lions.

reptiles: cold-blooded animals, such as lizards and snakes.

rodents: small, gnawing animals, such as rats, mice, and squirrels.

scrublands: land covered with stunted trees and shrubs.

snares: traps.

stalking: silently creeping up on a prey animal.

territory: an area that an animal lives and hunts in.

urine: an animal's liquid waste.

wildebeests: African antelopes with heads like oxen, short manes, long tails, and curved horns.

 # More Books to Read

Big Cat Conservation
(Science of Saving Animals series)
Peggy Thomas
(Twenty-First Century Books)

Life Cycle of a Lion
Bobbie Kalman and Amanda Bishop
(Crabtree)

The Lion Family Book
Angelika Hofer
(North-South Books)

Lion: Habitats, Life Cycles,
Food Chains, Threats
Bill Jordan
(Raintree/Steck-Vaughn)

 # Web Sites

Asiatic Lions
www.asiatic-lion.org

Big Cats
www.bigcats.com

Lion Research Center
www.lionresearch.org/faq.html

Oakland Zoo
www.oaklandzoo.org/atoz/
azlion.html

To find additional web sites, use a reliable search engine to find one or more of the following keywords: **African lion, Gir Protected Area.**

 # Index